Limbo

First published in 2021 by Blue Diode Press
30 Lochend Road
Leith
Edinburgh EH6 8BS
www.bluediode.co.uk

ISBN: 978-1-9164051-7-2

Typesetting: Rob A. Mackenzie.
text in Pilgrim LT Roman

Cover art: Germany, Berlin, circa 1930: LiliGraphie /
Shutterstock
Cover design and typography: Rob A. Mackenzie

Diode logo design: Sam and Ian Alexander.

Printed and bound by Imprint Digital, Exeter, UK.
https://digital.imprint.co.uk

Limbo

Georgi Gill

Blue Diode Press
Edinburgh

for Lizzie

CONTENTS

Day 4
Saturday 6 May 1933

Day 5
Sunday 7 May 1933

Day 6
Monday 8 May 1933

Day 7
Tuesday 9 May 1933

Day 8
Wednesday 10 May 1933

Day 9
Thursday 11 May 1933

Day 10
Friday 12 May 1933

ACKNOWLEDGEMENTS

Thanks to the editors of the following print and online journals who published some 'Limbo' poems with the same or modified versions of the text:

Abridged: 'Hypoxemia'
Far Off Places: 'In the Closet'
Abridged: 'Holding my Breath' and 'Mal de Debarquement'
Coast to Coast to Coast: 'B.L.'
The Honest Ulsterman: 'Limbo' and 'Hangover'

And to Eleanor Livingstone and her colleagues at StAnza International Poetry Festival who featured 'On the Cusp', on the festival website.

My thanks to Rob Mackenzie at Blue Diode Press for publishing *Limbo* and for his insightful suggestions. Thanks also to Jean Sprackland at Manchester Writing School for setting me the writing challenge which led to the first poem of this collection. I am indebted to Michael Symmons Roberts for his patient and meticulous tutoring and feedback during the composition of early drafts. I'm filled with gratitude to Annie Rutherford and Colin Waters for feedback on later drafts, coffee and encouragement, and to Gillian Shirreffs, Samuel Tongue, Sandra Kohls, Louise Peterkin, Suzanne Finch, Audrey McIlvain, Jane McKie and Jennifer Williams for their top writerly chat and advice. Deepest thanks and love to my parents, Jenny and Peter. To Lizzie everything and always.

The characters in the following poems are fictional but Limbo's events take place in the context of actual events that happened in Berlin in 1933.

The Institut für Sexualwissenschaft (Institute for Sexual Science) was established in Berlin in 1919 and provided the city's residents with treatments for physical and psychological sexual disorders while also advocating for lesbian, gay, transgender and intersex rights. By May 1933 the Institute and its work was increasingly vulnerable to censure by the Nazi government's censorship programme.

Day 1
Wednesday 3 May 1933

Into Limbo

The best places are never in the best part of town,
the best places will always be shut down in crackdowns
by the police, the Party, the state, until we are left
with the shabby, the hit and miss, the hit and run, the best
of the not quite worst and we must make do,
must head down unlit stone steps,
we must dip into Limbo.

Hair indigo under club lights, B stands in the fringes,
black satin slick over pale skin, a body thin but toned.
B watches and is watched by strangers
pinching thrills in the shadows with boygirl girlboys,
while the kick-line holds its in-time, in-step poise,
its legs, the well-oiled, jerking gears of a machine.
Here everything is hidden but everything is seen.

A grey-faced businessman perches on velvet and muses
on a girl whose purple make-up accentuates her bruises.
A fat man, shiny and pink as a boiled pig, gawps
at a glimpse of nipple that tussles with a dancer's sequins,
while the vigilant digits of the cocktail waiter
finger the fat man's wallet for notes, and later
that waiter will acquire photos of that very same nipple
and sell them on to his victim.
For the Limbo Club is the place,
the very place for a hands off, hands on
hour or three of what you make it.

A short man steps onto the small stage;
each magnifies the other.
Bow tie, tuxedo, bare chest, fishnets. He has eyelashes
that a debutante would covet, and no, he is not afraid
of the liberal application of Blushing Rose rouge
to carve a pair of cheekbones from his jowls.

The house lights go down. The spotlight picks him out.
The master of ceremonies waits for hush,
waits for the audience to anticipate.

Then. He. Speaks.

Lorenz

Willkommen, meine Damen und Herren. Welcome,
ladies and gentlemen of Berlin, navvies and the navy,
Nazis and Jews, drag queens and dykes, settlers,
squatters, blow ins. Let me guide you. Allow me if
you will to be your seducer, your confessor, your
factotum. (Yes madam, I can do everything.) Explore
with me and we will offer you distraction, stimulation,
subversion, fragmentation, contradiction of everything
you think you know, connections, complexions,
addictions, fictions, an Egyptian with excellent
diction, short-lived affections, longer-term infections,
sedition, desperation, deviation, depravation and – sir,
I think your tastes incline to degradation. I guarantee
our show will give you satisfaction and I personally
give you absolution.
Here is everything. Here is nothing. Welcome.

Four Ways of Looking at B

After Wallace Stevens

B's hair
is the one vital flame
in monochrome Berlin.
A hiss of blue gas,
it can warm you,
but proceed with caution.

One can get used to anything,
but if B ceases to be new,
becomes as conventional
as cards at Christmas,
we are all undone.

B is an oboe note held
just a fraction too long.
When it fades, you realize
the air was always too still.

The vocal in that song you like –
background oohs and ohs and wohs
that are both joyful and fearful and woeful
in perfect accord? That is B.

Curious

B senses attention; sends sidelong glances
back at a woman, a blowsy woman
lolling in a fog of cognac and sweet perfume,
hair teased into a cloche of loose peroxide curls,
flesh sausaged into emerald satin,
spilling out like a punctured Bratwurst on a grill,
tipsy eyes idling over B.

She would sniff B's collarbones,
would trace their trail with her tongue,
would forgo her beau to trace B further,
trace B deeper. Would bare a breast
for a glimpse of chest. Imagines
what lies beneath B's waistcoat,
what lies beneath the trousers, so snug,
so fitted over slender hips. Would know
what lies beneath. Would spread her legs
to investigate the rumours she has heard,
to investigate this desire to go deeper.
She settles for tonguing her own lips,
touching, tasting by proxy, tracing
a smear of scarlet lipstick across
her own pan-stick chin.

Cognac, a sniff of cognac is a smelling salt,
prising the blowsy woman back from herself.
Her beau has returned, slopping brandy
on his jacket, splashing his Party badge.
She looks down and snaps her legs together.
B nods and smiles and knows the type –
merely curious among the curios.

Fuchs's Observations in Limbo

'He listens well who takes notes' —Dante

This is the edge of hell,
where human dogs piss their sins
in stinking puddles
on the floor.

Every third beat of the music
is fractionally off, and the double bass
has gone astray, but still the chorus struts
its ragged line.

The tall girl at the end – girl? Yes, girl –
her dress, pimped by this place, slips,
declares her jingling nipple without
a hint of shame

as she keeps on, legs pumping, hips
grinding. She could fuck the very oxygen
out of the room. And the dance floor:
that is not dancing;

that is fully clothed fucking. Women
are pleasure-palace whores in this labyrinth
of queers and tarts and dealers.
Just one person,

slim and taut as a whip, hair indigo,
holds back, eyes blank as a cat,
self-discipline in the face of total
surrender to sin.

A blue-eyed officer, jacket unbuttoned,
is coarsened by an M.C. in corset and stockings,
stroking his thigh. Oh my, this party could
bring down the Party.

Casting About

A nimble surprise, the pig-faced man switches
a banknote for the photo in the waiter's hand.
One fluid move. Fuchs fakes this taste
for dancers and their disembodied nipples,

but he has to start somewhere with someone
and the waiter-pornographer-wallet-lifter –
perhaps informer – might just help the hunt.
Fuchs, the pig-faced man, does hunt, is adept;

can pick off the weak without raising his pulse,
and the herd here is oh so weak, so sick,
so very predictable. Except one, the odd one,
the aloof one, holding back like a bank vault.

He senses bigger game so plays a longer game;
recruits the waiter, who, he learns, is called Hans,
is handsy. Has secrets of his own. Yes, Hans
will help him out. Of this Herr Fuchs is certain.

Day 2
Thursday 4 May 1933

An Arrangement

B's landlady, Frau Jung
(touching seventy if she's a day)
is skimping on coal for the stove,
scratching out pork skin and crumbs
for her cat, but Mitzi and B
have come to an arrangement.
Mitzi in a new role – a living stole,
a warm touch, a soft touch, bartered for access
to a nightclub storeroom, stocked with mice.

A murmured invitation and Mitzi curls
over B's overcoat, around B's shoulder.
There is something regal about Mitzi;
shining white fur, slender, accessorized
with black socks, black ears.
There is an elegance about B;
tall in dark wool trousers, all legs, edges
and cat. Upright. Proud. Understated.
Through the door to Nollendorfstrasse's
shock of cold, its slick, tarmac river.
Mitzi harrumphs, then settles for the best
she can get, settles deeper into a coil of collar.

Stepping Out

This is not the time or the place
to settle. There is not an air of menace –
no, not as such, but like the drizzle
that glances off windows and kerbs,
B skims the crowds – knows now
is not the time or place to stick around.

Charcoal hat drawn down, close and taut,
the scene is cast in greys from sky
to shoes, save the odd flash
of electric blue,
sparking under B's hat.
But you'd have to watch for that,
be alert,
be on lookout.

And everyone might be on lookout –
probably not – but 'might' can slip
to 'may' to 'would' or 'should',
then skid to 'probably', 'definitely',
'must be',
'is'.

Don't stare at passers-by straight on,
point blank, dead true. No.
Head down, keep moving, straight on,
get gone.

There is nothing to see here.

The Institute

Das Institut für Sexualwissenschaft, Berlin,

Antiseptic Lysol scours each nostril,
rubs out the stench of hate that remains still,
prescribes instead: *Knowledge; Progress; Science.*
This formula, this prayer against bias
intones from stark, white walls in thick, black type,
like a harsh-toothed nit comb on blistered scalps.
Each door could shut out wary newcomers
with its weight of procedures and rumours.
Meek-kneed, B wavers between bolting home
and compliance, craves outside's humdrum fumes.
Yes, here everybody will be welcome
but not everyone will want to come.

For the Professor B Becomes

a text to be studied, deciphered, annotated
a novel element for the Periodic Table
a language to be translated, voluble on the tongue
a domain to be claimed, explored and mapped
a guide to lead him to illumination

Exposure

B's robe, a thin cotton pelt
is peeled off, scalped onto the floor.
Face forward.

The flashbulb burns, fizzes.
Time sags, tenses, sags.
Breathe out.

In profile, flesh cambers
into dips, then arches in pale
new moons.

The bulb burns, time spins out
river-wide; snaps back.
Breathe in.

Legs spread, chrysalis and butterfly
wings are caught together, pinned
on film.

The flashbulb burns, fizzes.
Time stretches like frayed elastic.
Breathe out.

Mounted, framed and filed,
the documenting of B
has begun.

Hat-check

Bad hair, bad skin, bad teeth, a ready smile,
Laura, the hat-check girl leans across the counter.
Laura is merry, perhaps too merry,
as she tells B her best dirty joke,
the one about the Nazi and the sheep
taking lunch in the Tiergarten.
B knows the joke but laughs
as if the punch-line hits home hard.
Knows that Laura goes to the Tiergarten too,
knows that Laura is being treated for syphilis,
knows that Laura used to be a dancer
before merry became too merry.
Knows Laura wants something in return,
the gaps in her chat as wide as the gaps in her smile.

Midnight in Limbo

The punter lumbers after the showgirl,
weaves across the dance floor to the bar,
never tires of the sparkle of her giggle,
the babble of her sequins louder
than any other dancer.

'Giselle, Giselle, Giselle
means word of honour.
Do you give me your word?'
Giggle, nod, giggle.
'Giselle, Giselle what is your word?'
'Champagne!'

On the counter two coupes hiss and spit,
pestering to be drunk and drunk again.
Two glasses of cheap sekt chime a toast,
two prayer bells that ring in assent,
wine fizzing, splashing, blessing patent toes,
hallowing this impatient, thirsty tryst.

Day 3
Friday 5 May 1933

B, Nollendorfstrasse, 10:47am

Behind the locked door, I breathe and stretch,
turn to the single-ring stove by the window,
make the gas sigh and strike a match.
They are precious, these private hours before Limbo:
the quiet percussion of spoon scraping coffee tin;
the kettle singing, climbing the scale unchecked.
There is time enough for this before my day begins.
Behind the curtain, I view the street's aspect
of rain-damped concrete and there suspect a shadow
swells darker than it was before, see the subtle
glow of a freshly lit cigar linger below.
I watch, sense that I might be some hunter's truffle.
The kettle shrieks and burns off my doubts:
I know I am quarried, snuffled, rooted out.

Fuchs, Nollendorfstrasse, 10:47am

I could sniff out the secrets of this whole building,
discover each unfaithful thief or slut, but my skill is in
the discernment of the diamonds from the paste.
My inner eye knows it spies true prey in this place:
a shadow thrown against a third-floor net curtain –
there in a shabby bedsitting room, I am certain.
Rising late, stretching. Dressing? No. Dishabille.
Unaware that in private much is revealed,
B stoops, bends to what? I sense no lover here
but catch the brief blaze of a match on the air.
and I light up too, send smoke rising between us,
infiltrating B's air, scouting out B's weakness,
while I fillet information from the neighbours.
If you wield the knife right, friends will turn to traitors.

Examination

The tape measure spools loose, then pulls tight
to cuff, to capture the circumference
of torso, hips, thighs *81, 64, 84,*
centimetres read out, relayed to the nurse's
careful black pen, clinical routines unabashed
when faced with difference. Legs fanned wide,
B observes this inspection, this examination
of flesh, winces at the chill of a caliper
horseshoeing an unnamed organ,
seeking definition, seeking precision.
B senses external discomfort, feels the nurse
frown at the almost inadvertent eyeful
that drives her further behind her clipboard,
Eyes clenched shut, B lies back and is explored.

Consultation

The Persian rug is a no man's land between us,
an unclaimed territory of tufted threads
woven into the Tree of Knowledge,

its trunk, rising from the blood of the red border,
branches twisting out of the darkness, bursting
into leaf, many leaves, but barely any fruit,

small, dense, shrivelled. I could choose to talk,
spill my guts all over the Tree of Knowledge,
let my words plant the seed for another fruit to ripen,

but the air in the room is thin. It waits to be refreshed
with breath and voice, hard consonant facts, the rounded
vowels of memory. How can such emptiness hang so heavy?

The Professor, clears his throat, testing the acoustics,
a crackle warming up the wireless. His voice paces
across the rug, 'B, tell me about your childhood.'

Chimera

My father was a tall man, skin tough
as a razor's strop. He shaved with care

at the kitchen table while I held up the mirror.
He said I had too much to be a woman,

not enough to be a man. Prayed each night
for God to cast a dense veil of shame

over my flaws. A well-meaning man
but not well-read. Mother, hands in lap,

sat silent. She had studied Ovid: knew the danger
of petitioning the petulant gods; recognised me

as her Hermaphroditus, her own living myth,
her carelessly glued together child of legend,

her chimera. A dandelion growing bright, defiant,
on the manicured lawn, I was not born for the suburbs.

No, she told me, better to get out, find a fairy
tale, live there or, failing that, Berlin.

Benediction

The Professor's hand on B's shoulder,
firm and light, this summation, this benediction.
'You are neither this thing nor the other.
And no, not half. You are one perfect coalition.'

The Determined Hour

Eight in Limbo marks the determined hour,
a crowd fixed on mixing with the debauched,
with the clock-shy louche who won't get here
till gone eleven, sloping in as the pretenders,
tipsy Cinderellas, head home.
For now, the determined sit and drink,
noisy, nosy, gawking from table
to table to look-see
if anyone gapes back at them.

Just a bauble on a table, a miniature
Dachshund licks from a martini glass
of milk, is petted by a gaggle
of women, frowsy, tousled women,
cooing in shrill, blonde tones.
Benevolent smiles and sharp creases,
a man in officer's uniform,
paws the women as they paw the dog,
clicks fingers for the waiter
and a round, then another,
of brandy Alexanders.

Humans and dog lap up
their milky drinks, as the officer
tests flesh with a connoisseur's
arrogant grasp and squeeze, plumps
for the skinny blonde, the drunk redhead
as rewards for a week's hard work.

B, Limbo, 11:52pm

A chill air wafts behind me. Someone
stepping on your grave, my mother
would have said. I stand straighter,
each hair alert to movement, to danger.
Oh! Damp sausage fingers brush my back,
each fingerprint stains my flesh with sweat.
I am claimed, marked by an animal scent

as someone's territory. Not someone – some man.
My heels lift from the floor. I want to run
but volte face to face him, the pig-faced sneak,
his lips stealing my air. I know him by sight
but what does he know of me? Lecherous breath
scorching my skin, he grins as I grip myself
together, my face a penknife snapping shut.

Fuchs, Limbo, 11:52pm

Tonight there is temptation: B's shoulder blades,
flawless, defenceless, flaunted by a backless
frippery. I cannot resist a lick of my fingers,
a trail across flesh and lace, lace and flesh,
soft, rough, rough, soft to my fingertips,
a whisper of a touch, just enough to surprise,
to disarm, to alarm.

Static air fills the space where B, now a pistol,
recoils from my hand, spins round to face me,
in this heartbeat, vulnerable as a shaved cat,
then, too late, eyes narrow. My fingers
still tingle from the contact, from the certainty
that they belong to the upper hand.
Guten Abend, B. We should talk.

Intermission

'Entschuldigung, mein herr! Excuse me, sir.'
Lorenz, a fluster of ruffled satin, takes centre stage,

comes between Fuchs and B,
his face a mimeograph of regret.

'B, une petite crise brews backstage.
Verzeihung, mein herr! Veuillez m'excuser.'

Fuchs catches a scent of scandal
behind the curtain. Sniffs, licks his lips.

Lorenz simpers, shrugs. 'Worry not, sir.
Chorus girls will bicker over stockings.'

Lorenz hustles B behind a screen,
past three dancers rehearsing

– side to side, misstep,
and take it again from the top –

to the temporary refuge of a damp mop closet.
He lifts a finger of one thousand

tiny tendernesses to B's forehead,
caresses the point between

pencilled eyebrows. Blesses B.
'You are the rarest of delicacies,

mein Liebling. Beware.
He will use you to trap us all.'

B.L.

In order to construct a habitable home
from loneliness, you must be confident
that you can anchor yourself to a strict timetable.
Do not squat, open-mouthed and hungry,
in the unpredictable minutes and hours
lying vacant or, worse, vacated by a stranger
who might have become a friend. To get by,
tally the often overlooked, the small change
of each scheduled task: the number of sips
in your morning coffee cup; how many paces
from flat to street. Know the exact measure
of an amicable arm's length required to fend off
the eager grasp of other lonely people.
B knew all of this; had practised it with the dogged
concentration of a devoted monk, in the years
Before Lorenz.

Day 4
Saturday 6 May 1933

Die Zuweisung

Bad hair, bad skin, bad teeth – Laura, the hat-check girl folds in on
   herself,
shrinking into frayed threads, half-chewed up, a discarded hostel
   breakfast.

She spots him. *Sauntering, spivved up, devious bastard.* Hans slows,
slows, stops. Starts strolling. Glaciers move quicker than this.

Hair crackling in the chill air, jumpy as a terrier, Laura watches,
curses, watches his meticulously carefree saunter. *Bastard.*

Feet a smudge on the pavement, tethering her down like a weight
on a balloon, Laura fumbles a fist of notes to Hans, a fist of tips,

of tip-offs, of thefts, of backroom fumbles, all for just one fix.
Hans sways a limp hand. *Bis bald. See you in Limbo.*

But Laura has disappeared into the shadows at the edge of the alley.
Laura is dissolving into weightlessness.

Pilgrimage

Hans strides out, dodging needles of rain, heads
to his cathedral, Wertheim's department store.
Such bright opulence. Such magnificence.
Such affluence that, on the rare occasion,
Hans is grazed by ambiguity, by the possibility
that something of him is tawdry, tainted
by association with the wretches of Berlin,
on this very rare occasion, Hans goes to Wertheim
and makes his confession, bows, pleading
for redemption at the benevolent altar
stacked with solid gold Cartier watches.
But today Hans leaves prayers to the addicts,
to those condemned to be in greater need.
Whistling a showy tune, he seeks a gentleman's
umbrella and new shop-girls to put to work.

For Mitzi B becomes

a novice, learning to tread softly and leave no prints
a fellow nocturne, gliding through the darkness
a comfortable silk cushion, made for drowsing on
a limousine that conveys her to dinner
the keeper of the mice

Saturday night

The members' room of Limbo
is like living inside the chamber
of a heart, pulsing red.

Against the inky dark Malbec
of the wall leans a woman
in a velvet dress the colour

of Pinot Noir, the colour
of hot blood, curving full-bodied
across her bust, a jarring

almost-match with her hair's
long, dry Merlot and the tobacco-
scented Cabernet Sauvignon

of her thin, puckered lips. The air
is stained tempranillo so only
her face stands out, pallid,

disembodied; a blank, sallow moon
with black crater eyes
that survey all

but serve whom?
She watches, catches B's eye,
a dory hooked and glittering,

hanging on one stuck breath
until the watcher casts her eyes
wide and B dives deep into shadow.

For the customers B becomes

a lodestar lighting their course through Limbo
a whirl of teeth and gossip
a new beau, an old friend, but no –
a mirror, cold and unresponsive to touch
a full stop that punctuates the end of their day

One-sided

It's a darling little club. Needs new faces,
fresh blood. Just the spot for the likes of us.
You know the thing – all gin, jazz, long vowels
and leather. Bread and butter to you and me, dear.
Just our cup of tea –
                              – well, call me back.

A friend of a friend has a friend in London –

You do know Franz –
he can set us up in Paris or Lausanne.
Tour to the Eiffel Tower,
trek through the alps.
Well, not trek, but breathe
safer air. He –
                    – well, call me back.

Who says?

Lorenz, we can go somewhere better –

Anywhere better –

Anywhere.
Call me back.

Reflection

Lorenz faces himself, gazes, appraises,
sees what the blue-eyed officer sees in him:
eyes, cloudless and wide; hair, thick, boot-polish black;
lips full, not slutty but, well – yes – slutty.
Trails a glue-stuck matchstick across his eyelid,
then snares a caterpillar of eyelashes,
fingers tamping the black strip firm to one eye.
Presses. Pauses. Levels with the mirror, views
one eye monocled in glamour, one narrowed,
nude, the whisper of a crease puckers its skin,
and he knows the clock will now accelerate,
sees himself balding in a bedsitting room
or worse. Shudders. Blinks. No. Lorenz will focus
on his officer; be what *he* wants to see.

Day 5
Sunday 7 May 1933

The Landlady

Bulky as her Biedermeier mahogany
wardrobe, Frau Jung is reassuring –
too valuable for firewood, but too old hat
for now. Stubby legs, ankle-skimming
skirts: last century's bed that once graced
the honeymoon suite, she is sagging
where her springs have sprung.

Faithful to the good old ways,
yet she concedes to the need
for occasional paying guests.
And yes, her eyes are sometimes shut
for a quiet life, if tenants pay the rent
in full, on time, and bring no
3 a.m. disrepute to her door.

Better than her neighbours,
she never thought to trade in talk.
But, at the butcher's, she rootled
for coins to buy two pig trotters,
and had a furtive taste of steak,
courtesy of the well-dressed stranger
who spied she'd had a bellyful of hunger.

For Frau Jung B becomes

a secret stored in the fatty folds of her brain
good silk stockings at the back of the drawer
stolen cash beneath the floorboards
an insurance policy, as yet uncashed
an ace to be bid when the hand is right

Holding my breath

Just remain at home, curtains tight against the light,
bolt the door to all-seeing eyes, leave the key, heavy
and snug in the lock, a snub to those who would kneel.

Even slippered, Frau Jung treads heavy, impatient,
pacing the hallway, forced gaiety and offers of toast
to smoke me out, to trip me up with prattling.

No sudden movements. I mustn't wake the floorboard
that barks at my weight. Live as if I don't exist.
Do not disturb the dust; let it gather round me, on me.

Remain indoors, barricade my mind, keep safe
my keepsakes, memories of the place where,
the person who – shush. Stop.

Don't divulge the barest details, don't indulge
the pleasure of a name rolling around on the tongue.
Muffle all echoes. Leave no trace.

Hold my breath, crouching on this bed in case they hear
– who hears? – my lungs' slight move. What is wrong
with breathing? What is wrong with *me* breathing?

The half-silk and the grasshopper

An idle thought floats through Laura:
it is better to be a half-silk than a grasshopper.
Grasshoppers are always crouched in the dirt,
scuffing up their knees and chowing down,
but a half-silk is half-respectable,
half-hat-check girl and only half-whore.

Wear your silk half-right
and people won't notice the rest is rayon,
or, if they do, Laura has learned
that even rayon can distract the desperate
from the darkness.

Rayon: French for 'beam of light'.
Light bouncing off her Seductress lipstick,
lingering over the low-cut scarlet blouse,
a spotlight on the flesh flashing beneath.

Lit well, the world won't notice the black eye,
the choker of fingerprint bruises –
calling cards from the punters.
They won't see the punctures
dotting her arms, won't see beyond
the promise of a brief good time:
like grasshoppers rubbing bodies
in brisk repetition until they groan.

'Half-silks': a term given to occasional sex workers in 1920s-30s Berlin, often secretaries, shopkeepers, and office clerks supplementing their incomes. 'Grasshoppers' were streetwalkers who performed oral sex in the Tiergarten.

Day 6
Monday 8 May 1933

B becomes inconspicuous

stays in the shade without being shady
stands tall but does not appear to volunteer
speaks in a low voice but says nothing
tries to exist but not be missed
is evasive as a feral cat

The Pergamon

Blind-eyed statues stare:
I stare back – a game I play
to lose – stare, and blink first

but in all else I am stone;
I have learned to hold
myself in, and not give an inch.

I sense movement, atoms,
disturbed, shift in the air:
he is not far behind

in that other game, the game
of chase. In the daylight, dust
hangs. Statue dust?

Dust of me? Of him? The slow,
slow rot of skin is faster still
than marble's glacial crumble.

He huffs, shuffles, is bored.
He tarnishes the air some more
with hot breath impatient for the kill.

Monday Afternoon Cocktails

2 ounces of gin,
another 2 of soda water,
a half of blue curacao,
1 firm squeeze of lemon,
(better lime if you can get it).
Muddle everything and serve over ice.
Sip or gulp as required:
one Afternoon Blues.

An aperitif for the week ahead;
a digestif to settle the week just gone;
a ritual, a bribe, a stolen sacred hour:
the two of them every Monday at 5:00.

But today B waits, one glass half-drunk;
one, unclaimed, has lost its verve. 5:40.
A sip, a drag on a fag, a sip, the minute hand
lags its way around the bar clock-face. A sip,
a drag, 5:50. One glass lies sunk.
Waste not, want not. The second
is flat, blue, bitter. 5:58 p.m.
feels like 4:00 a.m. One sip,
and another, and spark a fresh smoke,
a sharp intake of isolation.

Wasted

B sees Laura slipping off her face,
off the face of the earth, slipping, sinking.
One eye swelling into a blue bruise,
she is hunched behind her counter,

> *I take the edge off,*
>> *take the sting out,*
>>> *no harm, no matter.*

Laura is here but not here.
'Liebling, you should take care.'
Ice in a glass, she is disintegrating,
daily, nightly, imploding, collapsing.

> *The stars are collapsing,*
>> *stars burning in space.*
>>> *Can I be a star?*

Sinking in on herself, just empty space,
Laura stands and stares. B can only try
to save her face with a tube of beige,
patted and smudged around the eye.

> *Dead star, blank star,*
>> *caving into my eyes.*
>>> *Hollow out my eyes.*

B cannot conceal, can minimize and does.
Laura does not flinch, is here and not here.
Two drunks drop hats on the counter and wait.
Laura stands and stares.

Booking

The first time they booked her was for novelty:
the mediocre dancer dressed in feathers,
bent double, arm extended
over her head in an ostrich shadow play.

The second time was to prove the audience
had indeed laughed the first time,
as she crossed the stage, spindly knees high,
parroting the bird's stop-start strut.

The third time was to plug a gap left by
the comedian, Gaggenheimer, who took his bow
one night then bowed right out of town,
forever more a no-show in Berlin.

The fourth time was to cover Willi Frankels,
the fifth Golda Hayum, both rumoured
to be in Paris, Lausanne, London
or the Weissensee Cemetery.

And now the cabaret grows thin, bare
as a hungry chorus girl. Yet it lacks bite,
toothless as your granny and why not?
There is enough variety off-stage:

the small hours tattoo of Party fists
on apartment doors; sudden arrests –
on vague pretexts; the clap of shots
in the street. Noises that make good people

barter with God to take their neighbours' lives
but save their own. And each evening
they must escape their silent betrayals,
burrow into the ridiculous, the familiar

strangeness of watching three times
a mediocre dancer dressed in feathers
bent double, arm extended
over her head in an ostrich shadow play.

Lorenz's apology for love

There's no harm in it – what I do to him and he to me.
To do what you want and not what you should
is the mark of liberty. I'm free, held in his soft hands,
such manicured hands; how bad can he be?
His worst crime is his try-too-hard cologne.
No, he just butters his bread with the Party,
sloughs off the grease with his uniform before bed,
my bed, hotel beds, beds at the flat of a friend.

There's no harm in it. We must take our pleasures
where we can. Peccadilloes or politicos:
choose what you don't want to see and what you do.
Turn a blind eye for a blind eye.

There's no harm in it. Indeed, there's champagne in it
and goose-down pillows to be pinned against
all weekend-long in the country. That's my boy!
Give me his strong wrist, circled in my two hands,
the feel of a silk tie, a nylon stocking trailed across
his chest and down. Give me his blue eyes,
clenched in concentration, then shocked open
in the surprise of a moment's release.

For Lorenz B becomes

the class you play truant from
the morning's insistent alarm clock
the glare of a Weimeraner long overdue its walk
the agony aunt's all too reasonable advice
the dis-ease before the doctor's diagnosis

Day 7
Tuesday 9 May 1933

On the cusp of meeting

I am waiting, staring, eyes reading the surface
of the tea that is cupped and on the table,
focus on the envelope of light rays
playing, reflecting, refracting.

A forgotten science class pitches into the present:
I recall this concentration of light is called
the *caustic* and imagine burning.

Staring deep, I travel in, in and become
the light rippling on the surface,
become this one infinite line.

It's inevitable: the curve cannot
straighten up but is condemned to bend,
and too tense, too long, I am on the cusp,
I *am* the cusp of bending back, of giving up.

Kaffeeklatsch

A poor forgery of refinement, Fuchs stands, bows,
'A drink? Something to nibble?' Licks his lips,

clicks at the waiter, places a silver cigar case
between them, its insignia a mutilated spider.

'Smoke?' B's head shudders no. A dragon, Fuchs's
nostrils exhale trails of smoke. B breathes in, a moment

to regroup, to affect a careful, slow yawn. Breathes
and waits, sips coffee. Seconds, minutes teeter. 'So?'

'Limbo. Fascinating, no? Irregular, no?' he says. B shrugs
a reply, 'People need to dance, to drink, to open the tap,

release a little steam. No harm in helping those in need, no?'
Cigar ignored, grey ash snows on the linen tablecloth.

'No, but also yes. I do not like to say deviant. Perverse.
Unnatural. I do not like to say these words to you –'

'So don't.' B's chair rasps back, telescopes one foot, two,
a mile. 'Well, there we are' – 'And where is there?' –

'Wherever we need to be and I need to be elsewhere.'
'An appointment with the Professor?' Fuchs expands,

B contracts, eyes fixed on the tablecloth, searching
for a secret hatch, an escape map woven into its nap.

'B, there are no secrets between friends, and a friend
of a friend let slip that you are a visitor to the Tiergarten,

to the Institute for Sexual Science to be precise.'
A most precise slip indeed. 'What other gossip

is spread by your friend of a friend?' Voice tight as a garrotte,
Fuchs licks his lips, 'Oh, my friend of a friend is very discreet.'

Mal de debarquement

The world lurches or is it my inner ears?
I am dizzy as a drunken sailor. The cobbles
shift, bend and warp, rising to meet me.
The streets contract to lanes then bloat
to boulevards, like the illusion of an oar
that bends in water, or a spoon melting
as it jiggles between finger and thumb.
Reality blurs the vision; my ears cannot
hold what they pick up in this out of control
city where the gravitational pull of wrongness
magnetizes citizens' sloshing minds.
A mannequin, I stand, eyes clenched shut,
stop my ears with fictional cotton wool.
The queasiness remains. Is it me
that is wrong or the world?

Fuchs dreams

I am alone as I dive into a pool, so clear, so cool,
so deep this moment of peace, and I feel,

I feel – but that is not me, no, that is B
and I am on the edge of the pool, grass nudging

my toes forward, urging me to plunge deep,
deeper into this liquid clarity and I see,

truly see B, oh my, I see everything, oh my,
as I float close, you twist and turn in the water

and, driftwood, I bob to you, with such sweet ease
I smudge myself against you, hand to hip, chest to back,

and, pond weed, I bind myself around you, close,
fast, dipping into you, souse myself in you, push

against the tangle of your limbs, your gulps
for air as you clutch the surface of the water,

struggle for purchase, for breath, as I pull us
                                        under.

B dreams

Words dribble from my mouth, letters spooling,
secrets, sins, facts, in stark bold type, hanging

in the air. I stuff them back, pinch lips to stop
my pipe and swallow, lock it in – every rumour,

every confession, each and every thing I said.
I thread a darning needle with coarse string

and begin – puncture my lower lip and wince
but press on, in and out through spongy flesh,

xxxxxxxxxxxxxxxxxxxxx I stich a row of tiny,
bloody kisses on my lips, sew faster, faster:

I hear his tread on the stair, tie off the thread
and am silent. I smell him close, sweat mingling

with the scent of blood, my blood, trickling
down my chin. The door is locked, the door

is open. He is here with scissors – no, shears,
huge and rusty – stepping forward, slicing.

Day 8
Wednesday 10 May 1933

Building a fire

It's a step-up from scouting for the youth league, this piling of textbooks, case notes, medical photos, porn, picture on picture: men on men; men as women; men who are not men at all; women with women; so many dildos! Unnatural scourges of society. One man, bent double, arse out for the camera, for the whip of a man in corset and laced-up leather boots, his face contorted with glee. Flushing crimson, the boys snigger, voices yanked down too deep for their bobbing Adam's apples. The officer drowns their work in petrol, in vitriol, teases their smooth, hot faces, bullies them and can, for they are passive in the light of the bonfire, in the light of their fierce desire to be in his gang, a desire that makes one youth itch, seduces him to rescue the whipped man, edges already curling in the heat, palming him into a pocket, saving him for later.

Auto da Fe

Opernplatz, 10 May 1933

The flames are assumptions of guilt,
shining a crude interrogation light
on the bonfire of Institute documents.

Even from this distance B coughs;
smoke dirties the throats of each observer.
Even from this distance B can sense

a replica B, feels tongues catching the gloss
of that other B on the pyre, twisting,
warping its Bness. Sudden hungry

flames raze each page of us; each record
of us; each photo; each and every expression
of us is extinguished by fire, recast

as smutty cinders that char and float,
float and fall, dirty snowflakes on the heads
of onlookers. We float, float, and fall

into gazing, gaping mouths. B knows
tonight we must swallow our cremated
selves and wonder what remains.

After the burning, B becomes

an empty jar, the label scrubbed off
a smudge of kohl on a lover's cheek
a half-forgotten, misremembered rumour
an unpicked seam of hanging threads
an ash cloud dispersing

Taking off

Blanketed by used examination gowns,
       dirty surgical drapes and bedsheets,
the Professor lies low, stowed

inside a laundry van,
       swaddled by stained towels, their stale damp
a defence against

sharp edges as he bounces,
       a lone ball ricocheting round a pinball machine,
with every swerved corner.

Like the heron flees its nest,
       the Professor has flown his Institute,
cut loose with a briefcase

stuffed full of notes
       (patient records and handfuls of francs).
He speeds across town,

swallowing hurried sips
       of sour air into lungs that thrum
to the urgent rumble

of the van's engine,
       and the Professor gags as queasiness
rises jittery in his gut.

Limbo

Tonight they drink cognac for shock
and champagne from habit.
Tonight there are no candles.
All who come are refugees,
seared by the soot outside,
scalded by the assault
on their ways of life.
No, there are no candles,
but red devoré scarves shield
stage bulbs that tonight –
for one night only – light
no acts but customers, the unsung
stars of a cancelled show.
Bitch fights and bar brawls
are truced until another time,
hushed by the all-night crimson vigil.

Fragments of arguments

'It's growing dark, getting late.
We should go.
We need to go.'

        'My go is close to gone
        so wait –
        tomorrow is here in...
        5,
        4,
        3,
        2,
        1.'

'We should go.'

        'Today might console us.
        Let the sun show mercy
        on Berlin.'

'A feeble sun...'

        '...burns brighter than us.
        Today may be lighter than before.'

'Our weight, light
as we are, lies in the timing.
We need to go.'

        'Time lies.
        Not now.'

'Soon, if not now, soon,
leaving will morph to fleeing.
Let's leave.'

'Now stretches. You know
it soon snaps back,
reneges, never buys its round.'

'Stand still and we corrode,
blister and erode
to nothing.'

'Don't go.'

Day 9
Thursday 11 May 1933

Hangover

Dawn strikes: Limbo evicts punters
into soft light, night hanging over
into day, cigarette smog clinging to clothes.
Kitten heels pinch grouchy toes and so
we straggle through the streets, loose threads
in morning's tapestry. Edges blurred,
abandoned party balloons,
we float in ones and twos
towards home, eyes cushioned
by veils of gin chiffon.
Sounds haze as if through cotton wool.
The world is too empty and yet too full.
We take this time to move, to pause
outside each other's double-locked doors,
to absorb the echoes of morning:
the sweet-sounding bickering of starlings;
the heavy grumble of the milk float on concrete;
the brush scraping fractured windows up from the street,
as the shopkeeper shores up his store, face ransacked;
and we pick a wary path, fragile to attack.

Red hot pokers

'Someone's got a new admirer.' A surprise
of flowers are thrust into B's hands. Doubt it.

Not here. Admiration does not extend as far
as Nollendorfstrasse. Petals spike, red-orange flames

too raucous for the apartment's muffled browns
and greys. Wary fingers pluck a card from the foliage.

B – you are excessive, de trop, besides the point,
surplus to Party requirements, expendable,

dispensable, redundant, unwanted by anyone
but me. Fingers burned, B slips the card

among the leaves. Frau Jung will not let the trail
alone. 'Lover boy or...' No. B throws a crumb

of an excuse, a smile, a shrug. 'Red hot pokers,'
says the Frau, 'Pricey. He's burning hot for you.'

Nausea rising, hot, cold, then hot again, B drops
the stems, stamps out their petal flames.

Hypoxemia

There is not enough oxygen,
not at home, not in Limbo,

not in the streets or the parks.
Men loosen ties, ease collar buttons,

just to get one good airy lungful
but the city has become cyanotic,

breathing in panicked gasps.
The streets are dizzy with confusion,

and everywhere is fatigued.
Front doors creak and drag,

feeble from the effort of being pulled.
Worn out from the heft, people wheeze,

purse their lips to buttress their windpipes,
just to keep heaving, keep breathing.

The Brandenburg Gate

Under the gate B waits,
is always waiting,
has always been waiting.
The who and how shift,
spilled mercury on glass,
but still B waits

for a friend of a friend
of a friend who has contacts,
who has papers, who needs
the money, who has no
sense of urgency.

Time moves on, slow as the sun,
to a new moment to – now! –
and now, and now the light
will fade.

B trails the rays, shadows swallowing
brick, mortar, brick and on,
until, under the gate, B is sealed
in an envelope of darkness,
such exposing darkness,
and waits.

In the closet

An aloof shrug in the bar swiftly morphs
into two too many Afternoon Blues,
into a broom-cupboard hug goodbye.
They inhale this moment, pungent
with eau de cologne, dust,
a stale damp mop, cigarettes and gin.

Lorenz kisses B: just one kiss;
a chaste kiss of painted lips
on painted lips, both contrite
and boozy; an apology; a pledge
of constancy; a memorial
to each anecdote, each snapshot,
each drunk party, each dirty joke
and every off-key song
they built their friendship on;
one lingering kiss between allies,
a kiss that refuses to say goodbye.

Day 10
Friday 12 May 1933

Wardrobe

There is no shame in stealing a dead man's clothes,
if they are well-cut from good cloth and his death
was not your fault. Lorenz takes heart from this, takes
the suit from the wardrobe. His landlord will not miss
it now. Double-breasted grey tweed. Those lapels
will bulk a skinny frame. Lorenz sees potential
for illusion – a costume, a character
who commutes from the suburbs with no detours,
no hidden affairs, no cocktails, no action.

Yes, this suit is subtle, subdued; indeed
it is a shrewd choice. He swipes shirt and shoes,
denies that a dead man's tie is unlucky,
even if you know he swung his way to death,
tells himself hanging is not catching like a cold.

Setting Out

The hunted must learn to hunt:
eyes facing forward as well as around;
focused on cunning as well as running.

B knows how to run the show, can construct
worlds from what others want to believe,
can believe in the confederate gloom of night,

but this curtain must rise in bare daylight.
B talks to Lorenz on the phone in the hall,
voice just loud enough to be interesting, just

tense enough to be a secret ripe for slipping.
Frau Jung's shoulders straighten, a soldier
on parade, tasked with some urgent errand.

In a moth-eaten fur and full greasepaint,
B tickles Mitzi's chin for luck and leaves,
patent shoes chattering down the stairs,

waves to shopkeepers, casts each one
as a witness, and walks towards the hotel.
The doorman of the Excelsior frowns at this

palaver of rouge and glitter, but steps aside.
Seen, then unseen, B enters, dips into
a basement cupboard and never comes out again.

The Stitch Up

1.
Lorenz takes one deep breath,
flings open the Excelsior café door
and pauses, takes on the role of himself.

2.
Polished mahogany boards:
the perfect dancefloor.
He appreciates a well-set stage,
the chassé past potted palms
and penguin waiters. A wave
to a charming chap or three.
Darling! You look marvellous.

3.
Heel pivot.
Bingo! Fuchs
sits opposite, hungry,
cornered in his trap.

4.
Lorenz sips coffee and waits.

5.
Taps his watch, shrugs and smiles
at Fuchs. *Mates and dates, always late
but what can you do?*

6.
An old man, myopic
in rain-spattered spectacles.
Mein leiber Herr!

7.
A snowdrift of tulle and feathers
cascading out of a garment bag
and over Lorenz, each stitch
considered and transfigured
into a dazzle of compliments
for Herr Becker, tailor
for the finest charades
in all Berlin.

8.
A Morse code of sequins,
a thousand tiny mocking eyes,
flash, dancing on the lacquer
of the empty table opposite.

Metamorphosis

The new passport is where forgery begins.
One must learn to pick its lock,
gain access to that which you are not,
put flesh on that which you have never been,
a stranger who may be dead or never lived.
So, B must learn to pick the lock of Bittan Ludwig.

Bittan means desire and B must desire
to be Bittan; must inhabit with precision
the state of maleness; apply just the right tension,
to wrench the voice half an octave lower,
increase its torque until the lock is sprung,
new facts tumbling smoothly off his tongue.

Success is lost or won in each detail:
B must file down any edges worn
sharp by Berlin to smooth Bavarian,
must allow the commonplace to prevail,
make believe truly in this artifice, all of it.
Only then will B be Bittan, a real counterfeit.

Walking in someone else's shoes

(*after Ciaran Carson's 'Revolution'*)

The policeman scanning the crowd with glaring torch-beam eyes.
The carping rub of unfamiliar shoes against my heel.

The officers, two by two, booted and superior.
The cobbles shining slick with rain? With piss? God's tears or
    blood?

The shopkeeper scratching at red graffiti with wire brush,
the slopping of bloodied rinse-water along the gutter.

The goose-flesh pimpled legs of the street girl on the corner,
the accusing bruise spreading purple from her eye to cheek.

The crooked antennae of an alert station clerk's ears.
The too firm, too fast, try-hard timbre of my new deep voice.

His sleight of chapped hands, nimble, conjuring notes and tickets.
The miasma of cigar smoke that creeps inside my nose.

The snap of a testy dachshund lunging towards my heels.
The departing train's stoked-up shriek of warning to us all.

Leaving, B Becomes

a newly encrypted message
hidden in a lacquered puzzle box

an airmail letter spit-sealed
posted and waiting to fly

a blueprint of bold lines
a new architecture for life

two fingers crossed tight
behind your back

The Border

West, west, west. The tracks chant,
leading us out of Potsdamer Bahnhof.
Teeming rain drives the train forward,
flushing us down the tracks and straight
out of town.

Legs wide, elbows sharp, I claim
both armrests and unfurl to fill my seat,
expand to fit my passport.
West, west, west. The conductor, damp
and chilled by station stops, stamps
through the carriage, stops, huffs,
clips my ticket. Moves on.

West, west, west. The train drums our way,
a steady heartbeat drubbing up from tracks,
through wheels, through carriage floor,
and rests, throbbing in my heels.

West, west, west. Suburbs wash into scrub,
west into fields, *west* into cities, *west*
until we halt at the border.
Footsteps sound, a shadow swells;
some person or persons out of view.
A guard fills the doorway. His fingers snap.
Dizzy, I hand over my passport,
this moment enlarging to hold my life,
to hold the world.

Georgi Gill is an Edinburgh-based writer and researcher whose poems explore a range of themes including the personal and cultural impact of illness and disability, and queer history. She often collaborates with other artists and writers on print, digital and performance projects. Georgi was the inaugural poet-in-residence at the Anatomical Museum in Edinburgh and she is the editor of *The Interpreter's House* magazine. *Limbo* is her first collection and was awarded the Michael Schmidt Prize for Best Portfolio.